- A COLLECTION OF POETRY -

The Cracked

Slipper

- BY DEANNE KIM -

Nebulae Productions and Booksellers CC.
P.O. Box 440,
Ngodwane,
1209,
Mpumalanga Province,
South Africa

Email Address: nebulae@xwi.co.za

ISBN: 978-1-77572-187-1

Layout and Design: Candice Pierce

Cover Design: Robert Mackintosh

For my daughter Candice, sister Maryanne and all those that have acted out their roles in this stage of my life's journey. Neil you too have been the strongest character in this play, a special thanks to you my "lost lover", may our paths cross one day as we journey into the Light and become Whole.

I give thanks to the Higher Powers and Light-beings for their protection and wisdom that they bestowed on us all.

- Acknowledgments -

Within this writing, whatever it faults, I express my gratitude to all those that have walked the road with me during my life's journey and therefore making it possible for me to express my inner feelings through these words

Contents

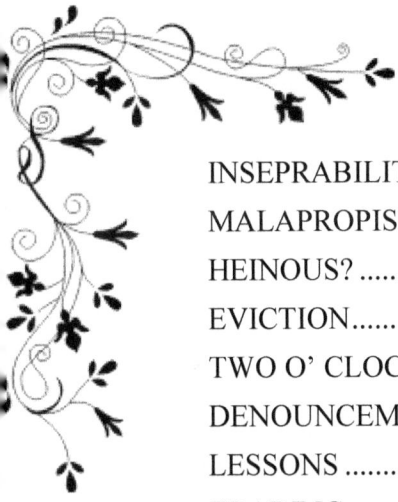

- *Prologue* -

These poems are based on feelings – "Real" feelings – my feelings and perhaps even your hidden ones too.
Life is not a bed of roses, nor is it one that you will live happily ever after. I started facing these realities a few years ago and then expressed them through the words that you are about to feel.

The greatest lesson I believe one can learn is to experience how we truly feel. To become conscious of our feelings, in other words to feel how you feel then express it, walk and talk it. Come to terms with who you *really* are, what it is you are *really* searching for, who that suffocated princess *really* is, and then allow yourself the choice of letting go. Fly - fly higher than you could ever imagine you would. Stop running away from the truth, have the guts to make the difference - one that suites you and nobody else. Learn to say "It's all about me!"
Your children will grow up - you did. Your husband might find a lover or escape into a world where he doesn't have to put up with your daily complaints. Start to live! Make it happen today. We are always postponing everything for that tomorrow that never comes. What happens if today you were faced with a mirror that showed you the truth, the truth about your

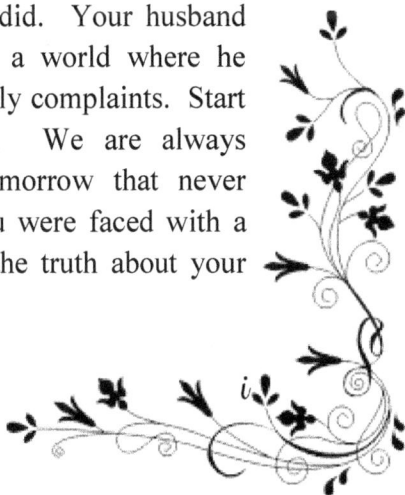

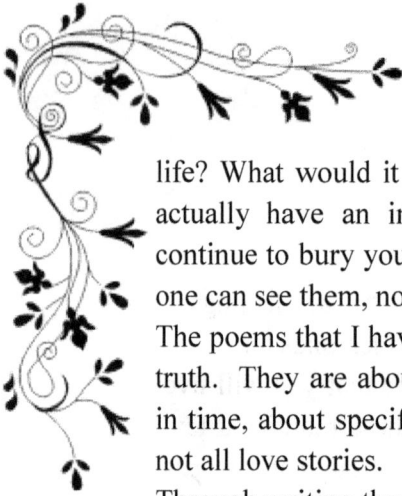

life? What would it be reflecting about you? Would it actually have an impact on your life or would you continue to bury your feelings under your skin where no one can see them, not even you?

The poems that I have written are about life, my life, my truth. They are about how I felt at a particular moment in time, about specific people and incidences. They are not all love stories.

Through writing these words I dealt with how I saw life, untied the wrappings and exposed the truth - my truth and now wish to walk and talk it.

Each day changes and so do you and me. What I felt yesterday might not be how I feel tomorrow - but none the less, all the words that I allowed myself to express are all memories, memories in time.

After wearing *the cracked slipper* for so many years - I can begin to right the wrongs; by writing from wrong I can now begin to walk my *truth*.

- *Biography* -

Deanne Kim, born and raised in South Africa, studied art for a total of 12 years. Art has taken her on a phenomenal journey, wherein she has taught formal art classes internationally whilst residing in the Philippines; as well as in her home country for a total of 20 plus years. Whilst studying through UNISA (University of South Africa), she branched into a new way of teaching, thus developed her 'Art Therapy' classes, which originated in Johannesburg in 1998. As an Artist, Publisher and 'Therapist', Deanne's love for children and passion for life has led her to write and illustrate educational books ranging from Grade R – 12, collectively resulting in over 60 Educational books produced to date. Deanne's zest for life, writing, teaching and passion never ceased after she was diagnosed with terminal cancer in 1993. Given a second chance has been the greatest gift and she wants to share what she has discovered with all whom cross her path. Through her own life's journey, she began writing and expressing her experiences –from this, she compiled two separate yet integrated books – *'When Cinderbella Gets Divorced'* and *'The Cracked Slipper'*.

- Part 1 -

1. *TIMELESS MEMORIES*

Whispering words of madness,
Silencing the acid air
With memories enclosed in a web of mind
As they deviously dispose their fears.

Noughts and crosses,
Snakes and dice,
Race to tie the knot
Of timeless memories.

-   (1997)

2. *EMBODIED.*

HAND
Tightly squeezed - no blood will flow.
Nails slice flesh - blood to glow
Cold – no life
Blood – the warmth.

TEETH
Locked together – no speech
Crushed – the sound
Pain – the silence
Unity – the freedom

EYES
Stare without vision
Blackness – escape
Dryness – emotion
Blindness – eternity

HEART
Anxious pulsation
Throbs the blade -
Beats the pain
I never really made.

-   (1997)

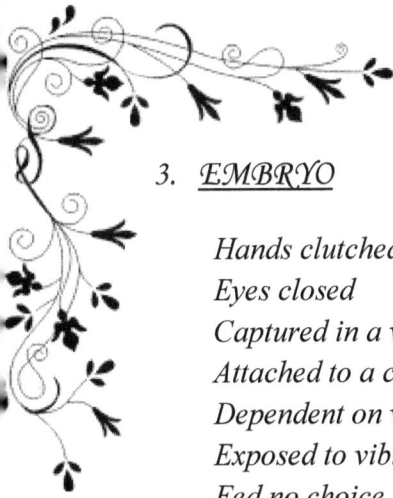

3. *EMBRYO*

Hands clutched
Eyes closed
Captured in a womb
Attached to a cord
Dependent on woman
Exposed to vibrations
Fed no choice
Incarcerated.

Escape my innocence,
Open my blindness.
Free my space,
Cut me loose.
Give me independence,
Unexposed to fear,
Feed me love,
Eternally.

-   (1997)

4. TO MY LOVE

You just don't understand
Why I feel like I do,
I need to be me,
I need to be myself,
I've been so like everyone,
For so very long.
Please understand just this once,
It's not that I don't want you,
To have anything you want too,
I only want to set myself free,
To be me,
Only for a while!

It sounds like I'm saying "I",
But it's important to ME.
"I" need to be the unique,
"I need to plat MY hair,
"I" need to run bare foot,
"I" need to be ME,
Please!
Only for a while!

-     (1997)

5. <u>LIES</u>

'Til death do us depart,
I surrender my all,
to love and to hold you,
and answer to your call.

We will never leave,
what we've joined together.
Hurts or hardships,
we will last forever.

Rings were symbolic,
as a token of eternity.
Jurisdictions now remind me,
of our lies of purity.

- (2007)

8. BIZARRE

Collecting,
Hoarding,
Saving,
Preservation perspires pompously our pride
and pains.

Stressing,
Exhausting,
Worrying,
Affirming anxiously the ambiguity of our
autonomous aims.

Working,
Laboriously,
Mechanically.
Pretentious proud paupers we pamper our paths.

Vandalising,
Destroying,
Wasting,
Mechanically mesmerised merchandise
we mime man.

Stealing,
Raping,
Lying,

Rectifying religiously ruptured rivalry of rights.

Mankind,
Vultures,
Thieves,
Slither sinfully silently into your insanity.

- (2007)

9. OH TO BE WED.

The prince never arrives
On that white horse
The toad
Never turned
into what was said
to be wed
is that of fairy tales off course.

Run maiden hide
Your little prince
Is dead.

Brides laden
in heavy white gowns
their future is harmonious
so they are told
life from this day
will offer them only
hardships and frowns.

Run maiden hide
Or your heart
Will turn cold.

They whisper sweet

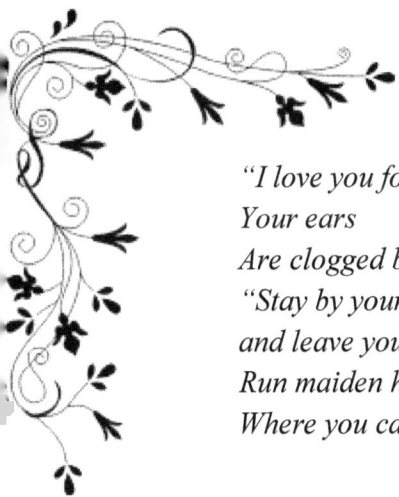

"I love you forever's"
Your ears
Are clogged by wax
"Stay by your side,
and leave you never"
Run maiden hide
Where you can then relax.

- (For my sister Maryanne. 2007)

10. THE FOOL

Tears flow like vinegar,
the mascara helps conceal my flesh
Where is the one I believed in,
or is it truly me that has changed our course?

Love does not exist
I'm beginning to learn that fast.
It lasts momentarily,
then evaporates back to its source.
Oh it's me that has changed
I should have known that of course!

Hugs strangle me
Kisses shut my mouth
Words deafen my ears
Lies engulf my pain
Love, life and longevity
Fade fast the words so faked.

- (2007)

11. RECONNECTING TIME

Time is like a thief
That vanishes into the blackness of the night,
Skilfully stealing precious jewels of life's breath.

We walked alongside,
You're much older now,
And yes, so am I.
Your arm around my aged body,
Time has passed us by.

Your eyes shine like virgin diamonds
Uncut by life's scars
Your blood is of mine
But your soul is ever free.

Where did time go?
You so silently became woman
Only yesterday I bathed and held you
To my breast.

We laugh
As we share
The memories of history
But silently
I suppress a tear
A tear that yearns

To hold onto this memory.

"Mother, my mother",
you whisper my name lovingly,
"Let time be time,
A season of death and birth,
Soon I will be same as you,
But for now let's stop
the stars and moon
Dance with me as we
Reconnect time."

- (Written for my daughter Candice while away
together. June 2007)

10. *BEING A PART*

I see
Your spirit
Dancing in the leaves
I hear
Your voice
Whisper through the birds
I feel
Your body's warmth
Glowing light from the sun
I taste
Your scent
On everything
I touch.

We are always together
Even when apart
Never hidden
By space or distance
For that is all a farce.

Look into my soul
Listen to the melody
Connect to our life's source
As we embrace the inseparable
Nectar of our unity

-   (June 2007)

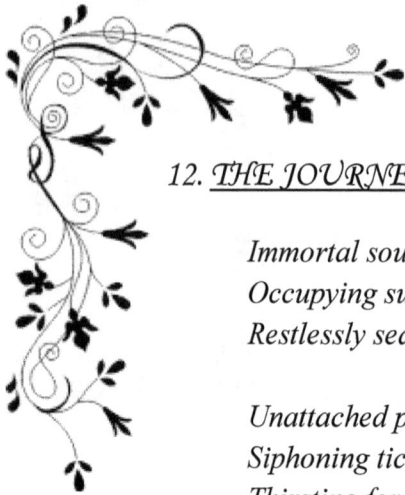

12. THE JOURNEY

Immortal souls
Occupying surgical homes,
Restlessly searching for fulfilment.

Unattached parasites,
Siphoning ticks,
Thirsting for life,
Yet never belong.

Voiceless sound,
Radiating coldness,
Like empty vessels
yearning for tangibility.

Chained heart
Captured by illusion
Beats to win this game

Tearful joker
Burns his gown
Only to discover
It has no colour.

- (2007)

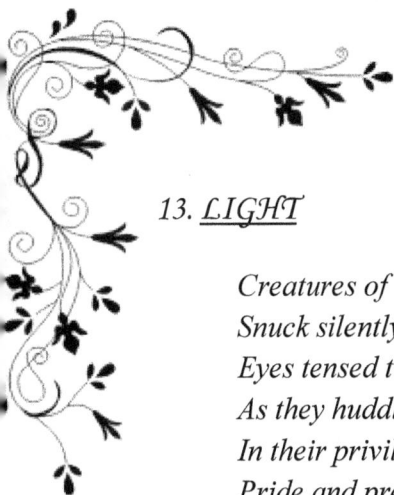

13. _LIGHT_

Creatures of darkness
Snuck silently in oneness
Eyes tensed tightly
As they huddle united
In their privileged
Pride and prejudice.

No mercy entered their minds
As they fought fiercely
For what was theirs
They were suckling' of sinners
And then,
Oh then,
God said,
Let there be light!

- (2007)

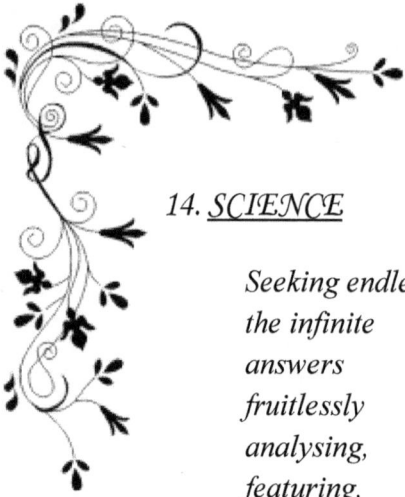

14. <u>SCIENCE</u>

Seeking endlessly
the infinite
answers
fruitlessly
analysing,
featuring,
questioning,
fanatics that seek
miniscule metaphors,
in space and matter.
never seize to
forfeit phantoms
that conquer their minds

-    (2007)

15. *THE PUB*

Veins like explosives
Limbs exploited,
battling beyond
bars baffled barriers.

Voices like ammunition
Sound exploding
barriers bewildered
bottled boisterously billow.

Synchronised like salmon
Swim captured.
Submarines slur
Simultaneously beyond bonds.

- (2007)

16. NEVER

Surely you would have known better
Than to belittle my pride
Humiliation - discrimination
No one can hide.

I'm hurt
Small
Nothing
Careless
Loveless
And yet I yearn for more

- (2007)

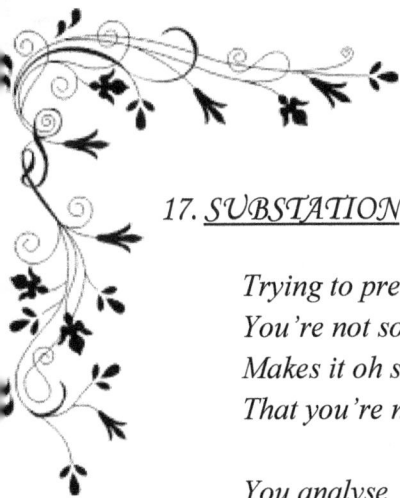

17. *SUBSTATION*

Trying to pretend
You're not so insecure
Makes it oh so obvious
That you're not that happy after all

You analyse
Criticise,
Mesmerise,
Pathetic hypocritical victim.

Grasp your situation
Find that match that sparks
the truth of your resurrection.

- (2007)

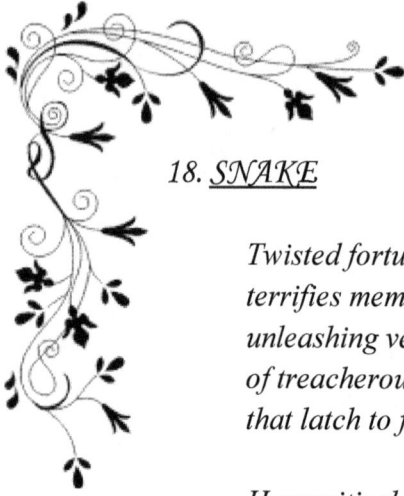

18. *SNAKE*

Twisted fortune
terrifies memories
unleashing venom
of treacherous fangs
that latch to fearful flaws.

Hypocritical sensations
slither momentarily
Monotonous motherhood
Umbilical connection
That attaches bond to blood.

Your venom
Saturates my veins
And still I conquer not.

Hissing whips
Strap my body not
Unleashed torture
Mesmerised in a non-hypnotised consciousness.

19. ONE WHO LOVES

One who loves truly
is always filled with the nectar
from his lover's flower,
the sap embraces his being with eternal warmth.
She nurtures his soul with sunshine
And feeds him with everlasting smiles of
reassurance,
That he and she are truly part of the wholeness of
Immortal love…
Forever

- (2007)

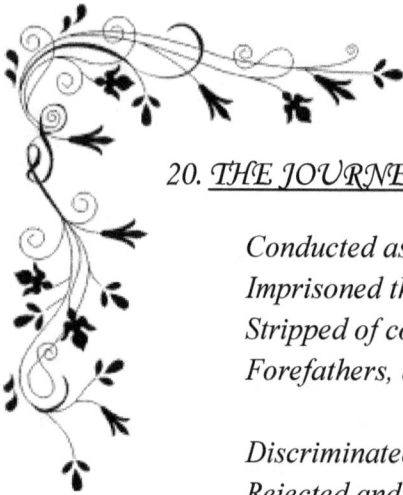

20. THE JOURNEY OF DESTINY

Conducted as slaves,
Imprisoned through accusations of falsity,
Stripped of country, pride and animosity,
Forefathers, ancestors come to our plea.

Discriminated for colour of skin,
Rejected and confined to boundaries and space,
Beaten and mocked because of features and face,
Forefathers, ancestors come to our plea.

Blasphemed as heathens for worshipping our
'gods',
Burnt at stake we suffered our turn,
Forbidden education in which we could learn,
Forefathers, ancestors come to our plea.

Destiny we hear will take its toll,
Life's wheel will spin full circle,
Horrors of past will reap their seeds,
Justice will therefore feed our needs.
Forefathers, ancestors will come to our plea.

20. BEHIND THE STAGE

Vulnerable body,
Nakedly exposed
Clothe me with your emotionless words
Your eyes have changed
They falsely accuse me of hopes
My passions enclosed by fear
Fear is not a word one can express
I cover it so deep,
now numb
Do you see my tears in your revue mirror,
While you drive me to drugs and drink?
Do I cling to hope of yesterday,
Or am I insane enough to act like all is right?
Actress, you will never find your fame
No one bellows your name
Shed your make-up,
Bleed in your own game
Tomorrow will be the same
Forget your frets
Only you, yes you are to blame.

- (2007)

21. INSEPRABILITY

Is it separation of body that questions our love?
Is it distance that strengthens our dreams?
Is it society's rights and wrongs that keep us
apart,
Or only our fear that mistakes are all the same?

When you're gone the distance is years
My dreams, reality
Night times are daytimes, I experience our dream
Memories of past melt away the pain.

In visions I call your name
Stroke your skin
Embrace your body
Smell your warmth
See your love
We melt primordially into the future
Shifting time and space,
A preview of things to be.

Proliferate our love
In this prologue called "life'
Fornication not forfeited
Desires not denounced
Forbidden fruits, sexuality and lust
Engulf this sea of love
Only dreams expose the above but soon
destiny's conception will propagate our souls.

- (2007)

22. MALAPROPISM

What are you incinerating,
Incidentally that the consequences of our
connection casually occurred by chance?
Is our destiny a purposely incommensurable
journey?
Are the incisions that I bear habitually refusing
to heal?
Is the turmoil of sound only an echo of truth
inside my head?
While terror of losing love unveils the whispers
of silence
Nullifying the insubstantial passions,
we regimentally both yearn for.
By denying oneself nothing,
Demented justice will demonstrate
A futuristic emotion of flaws
Notwithstanding the truth of delusion
We demise the collaboration of an evolutional
change.
Relieve my disordered distortion of life's
expectations
Inject morphine into my soul and pacify these lies
and delusions of sacrificial love

- (2007)

23. HEINOUS?

Praise be to thee,
Nonconformist,
woman
sacrificial saboteur
who ran the gauntlet
relinquished social security
recruited justice
cut the veil
on all cylinders
you burnt the books
smashed the glass slipper
and victoriously screamed
I AM!

Hail be to thee
Goddess of freedom
Unchained spirit
Who rides hell for leather
Life-giver of heads and tails
Exempt from sarcastic flies
And hypocritical corpses
They smother your dream no more
You are who you are
Purposely convinced,
immortal temptress.
- (2007)

24. EVICTION

Scrutinised by hypocritical prototypes.
brought to judgment
by those who detest disorder,
but clothe themselves in uniformed robotic
mannerisms
while imprisoning their hypnotised desires
against truth and woeful emotions.

Piety of life has determined my fate
to love another was to discriminate
conforming is pleasurable, so I'm taught
enlightenment toward derision denounced.

Plagued by militant masters,
Vultures of fame and acceptability,
Imprisonment my fateful state is announced
Pitilessly I escape death woes
And enter into an altered consciousness
to love another
Once more.

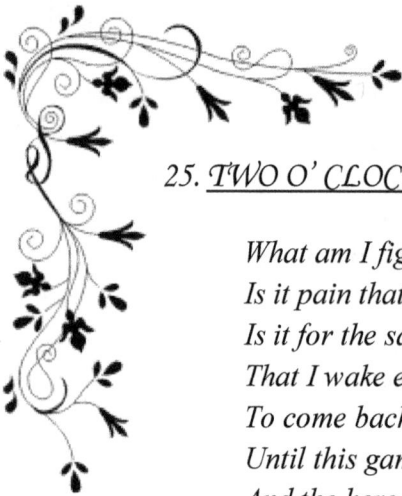

25. TWO O' CLOCK

What am I fighting for?
Is it pain that keeps my clock ticking?
Is it for the sake of believing in nothingness,
That I wake each morn
To come back for more
Until this game is won
And the heroes die in peace
Knowing that there is no tomorrow
No truth
No life after death
Only a fantasy of the yesterdays awaits their next
life
And yet in agony they yearn for more
 Hoping that the sun will fade their desires
And that their awakening will vanquish their
dreams of
eternal love.
 I surrender thee oh immortal fucked up sanity,
I forgive and forget that you ever allowed this
world
to dictate to me things of what to be, how to be,
what to say and how to live.
No more she cried, it is done,
I have learnt how not to live,
now set my spirit free,
to burn in hell eternally.
How could I have been so ignorant in this life?

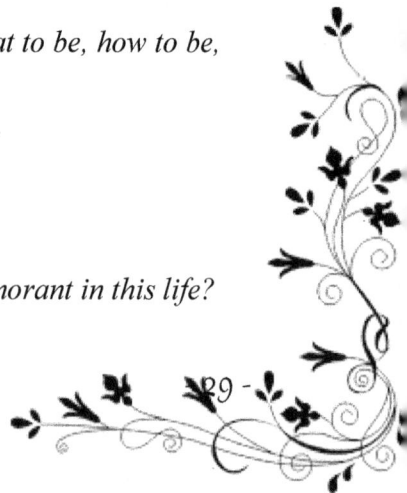

Sold my soul to lies,
Believed in make-believes
In love that never was?

Was it denunciation of one's self that gave
crucifixion its name?
Forgive me father I have sinned,
Now take me yonder to undo what I have done.

- (2007)

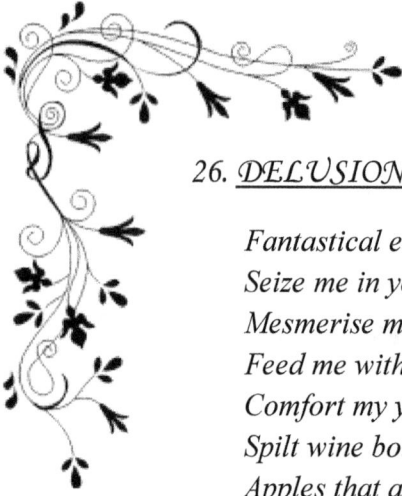

26. <u>DELUSION</u>

Fantastical error of confusion
Seize me in your comfort zone
Mesmerise me with your psychosis
Feed me with anxieties
Comfort my yearnings through emptiness
Spilt wine bottles that are labelled 'elite'
Apples that are acknowledged as sin.
What is it that I yearn for?

The pattern complete.

- (2007)

27. DENOUNCEMENT

Denial
Confutation
Unbelief
Dissent
Negation
Recantation
Rejection
Opposition
Refusal to accept it is happening to ME

.

- (2007)

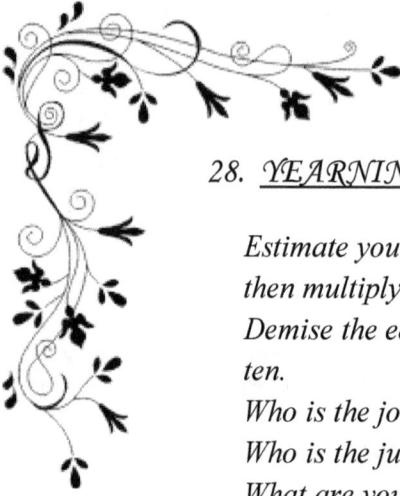

28. YEARNING FOR APPRAISAL

Estimate your fucked up state
then multiply it by nine
Demise the equation of sanity then divide it by
ten.
Who is the joker,
Who is the judge?
What are you aching for?
Who decides the verdict?
Why so many formulas
Contradicting the truth
Substituting reality
Momentarily in time.
Tuning into that emptiness
Equating the conclusion
Valuating segments of
Fragmented illusions.
Sustaining hope
Beating conditionally
Who holds the ruling?
You should know!

- (2007)

29. *LESSONS*

Life is a continuous struggle of reality versus
illusion
death and life,
faith before agnostics,
madness fighting sanity.
What is sanity?
Is it a forfeit of an illusory state of being?
or a reality of 'otherness'?
Does one declare denouncement of one's self
to be accepted into a mortuary of freedom,
or credible to be a part of the universal bank of
karmic freedom?
Who dictates the truth?
Who is worthy to be the judge of universal
energies,
that flutter systematically in non-existence
yet existed before time and space?
Parallel co-creators,
metaphors of life
yearning for the same cell
yet determine the conclusion as faulty.

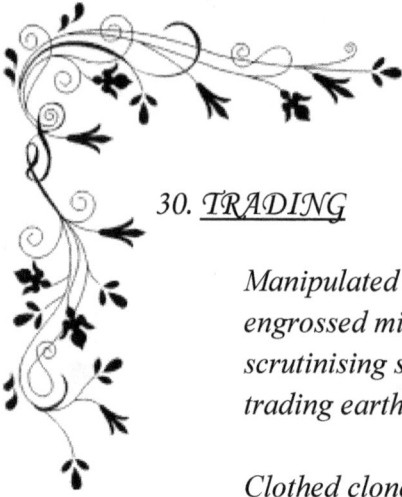

30. *TRADING*

Manipulated masses,
engrossed minds of fetish habitual falsehood,
scrutinising sensual lusts,
trading earth's seed for egotistical dwellings.

Clothed clones ever striving for insanity.
Hopes of heroism torments their saturated
desires.
Archetypical archetypes chipped and encoded,
they rhythmically march in pride,
only to discover that their destiny is death.

- (2008)

31. THE FIRST SUPPER

Excuse me while I disassemble your structured
setting,
unscramble the placement of your mantelpiece of
meticulousness,
Decipher your decanter vinaigrette and sip the
nectar of lifelessness –
Rearrange an array,
one displayed in darkness,
Untouched by humanities faults -
Flawless.

Excuse me while I shred your ornate cloth,
Repaint your starched narrow-mindedness,
Spill your etiquette,
compose new tongues,
Replaced by my interpretation of life's emotional
banquette,
Grounded in mud,
Perfected.

- (2008)

32. *BURNING FOR LOVE*

Dance with me in this flame
Where warmth and death are one
United essences of life brought forth
through surrender

Eternal immortal momentary lights
Swindling ruthlessly, forever.
Elementary pleasures combust as ignited love
Breathing the energetic night
Creating nothingness into ALL

Without you I have no flame,
Cannot dance,
Seize to burn
Wither into discarded ashes
which will lie on our earth and rot

Never forget that through life and death
You are my soul
You are my ALL
Only for one second come dance with me in this
flame?
Remember
Remember without mind
Don't judge our discrepancies
Forget the grudges
Throw out the bin
Be with this moment
And come dance with me in the flame.

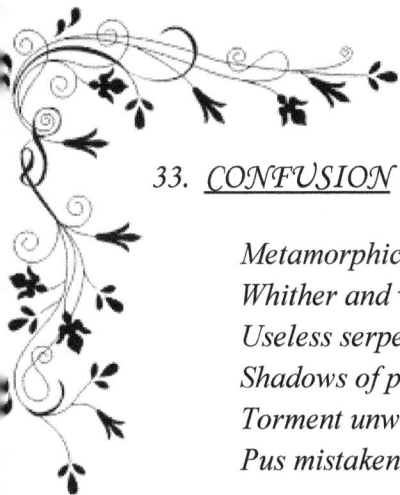

33. *CONFUSION*

Metamorphic residue
Whither and waste
Useless serpents and snakes
Shadows of past
Torment unwanted hibernated memories
Pus mistaken for icing

- (March 2008)

34. THE CHAIR

Life's constitutional legitimacies
Piled array
Splattered and shaped
by human mind

- (March 2008)

35. *DEPENDENT*

Lifelessly I clench to the ring that ties our bond
Loveless I stare into the space that occupies our
unity

Superficial saviour,
shallow lover,
you have become like a succulent cyst.

Momentary commitments
Now all ended
I walk
numb
into
colour
red

- (March 2008)

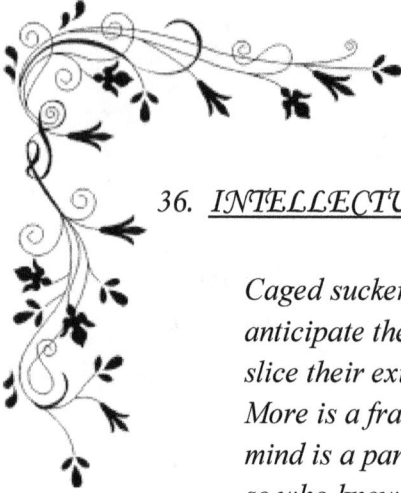

36. _INTELLECTUAL PEOPLE?_

Caged suckers
anticipate their unanswered thoughts,
slice their existence to find more.
More is a fraction of an explosive mind,
mind is a particle of all
so who knows why
and is why the all?
Is life about existing in the now?

- (March 2008)

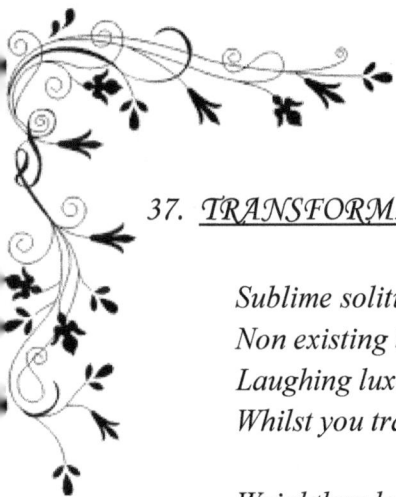

37. TRANSFORMING THE CATERPILLAR

Sublime solitude
Non existing being
Laughing luxuriously
Whilst you transcend time

Weightless larvae
Metaphorically
Returning
Majestically you capture
Uniqueness.

- (July 2008)

38. QUESTION

Ask about fears
and I'll flood you with darkness.
Ask about hurts
and I'll show you lifelessness.
Wipe away my mind
and I'll love again.

If mind is not matter
and life an illusion,
why pray for my soul -
why change its fate?

Are we not an immortal substance
of mind's fantasy
and deceived by perception?

Look into your own state –
fly into our togetherness
where we will confide
in our truth.

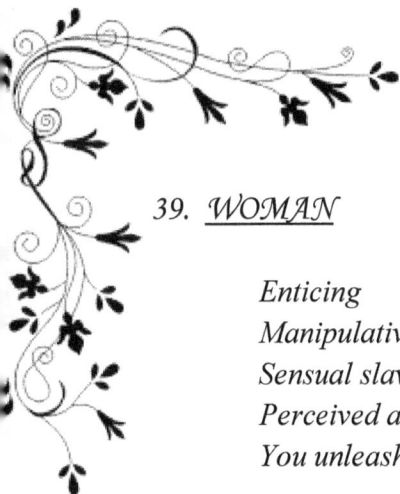

39. WOMAN

Enticing
Manipulative
Sensual slaves
Perceived as slut
You unleash their lies

Tempting muscular matter
the ruler of the game
skilfully slither inexorably to reveal
what is and what was
- oneness of kind

Behind clay mask - un-shattered stains
beauty behind
beauty beneath
always entwined
by matter of being

Ode be to thee
The Queen

40. *CHAINED*

Consumption my god
Undesirably I breathe

Anticipating
when
I
will
sense
the next
prick.

- (July 2008)

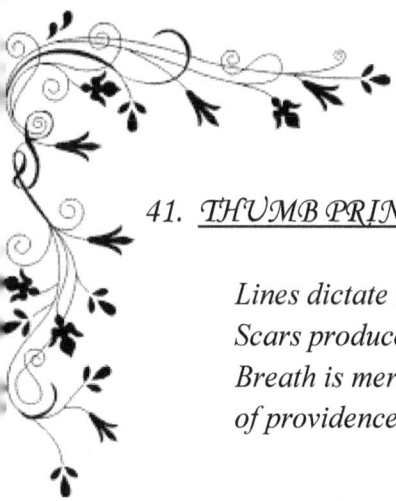

41. THUMB PRINT

Lines dictate the identity of uniqueness
Scars produce truth
Breath is merely an expression
of providence being exposed.

- (July 2008)

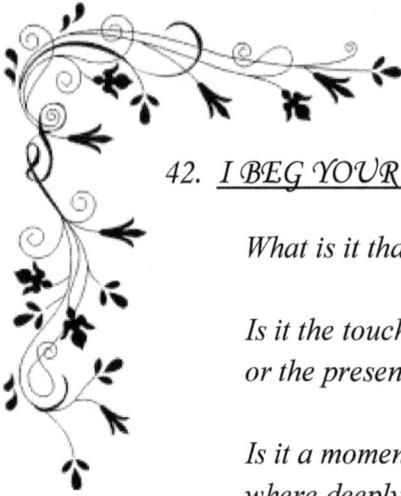

42. <u>I BEG YOUR PARDON?</u>

What is it that this human body aches for?

Is it the touch of another,
or the presence of self?

Is it a momentary lover
where deeply they know fades when the other
contractually resigns?

Is it for health -
while their bodies whither in pain?

Is it for serenity of acceptance that they know
will be annulled by societies new vote?

I wonder if life will ever gift human kind with
their makeup of reality and allow them to touch
the truth –
The very senses of soul's existence.

- (August 2008)

43. *AFTER THE LAST DANCE*

Movements of her shadow still echo in the icy air,
as she embraces her lost lover that once held her
so tight.

The silence
once sung

The lace
now torn.

Lovers disunite,
frowning resentfully
as they depart.

- (July 2008)

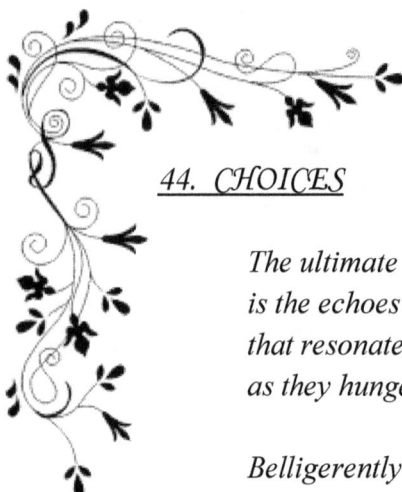

44. CHOICES

The ultimate of loneliness
is the echoes of voices
that resonate the mind,
as they hunger for love.

Belligerently they play out the rules,
while the Judge fictitiously observes and snarls.

Rights
what rights?

Love
what is love?

Mind
the conclusion of all.

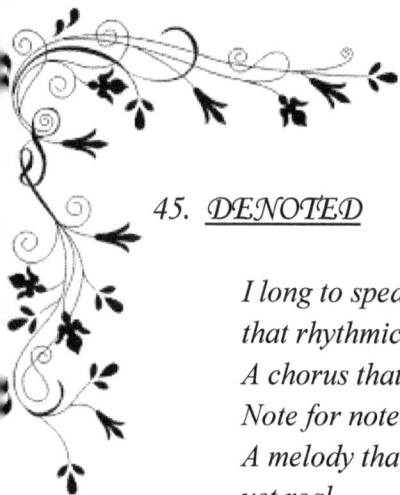

45. DENOTED

I long to speak the words
that rhythmically enchant my mind,
A chorus that beats loves truth
Note for note
A melody that is never played in human form,
yet real,
real only to the composer
of the tune. Noughts and crosses,
Snakes and dice,
Race to tie the knot
Of timeless memories.

- (July 2008)

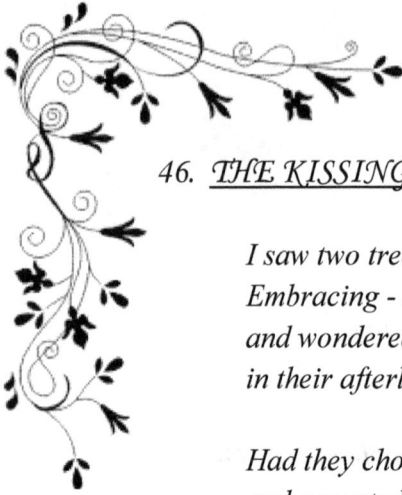

46. THE KISSING TREE

I saw two trees entwined
Embracing - they stood side by side
and wondered where their souls would lead them
in their afterlife.

Had they chosen this reconnection
and accepted their inseparable positions
to love and to hold the other
for better and for worse?
Would they only be altered
when death tore them apart?

- (Wedding Anniversary, August 2008)

47. *TELL ME*

Who do you trust
when you're yearning to verbalise silence?
Is it the stranger that smiles as you pass them by,
or the one that wears your ring?

Who do you hold
When your loneliness has left you cold?
Is it the shadow of the unknown
or the one that has let you down?

Who do you awake for
when your day is pre-designed?
Is it for the unpredictable,
or the one that ate your trust?

Who do you ache for
when your scarring has been sealed?
Is it for flawless lover
or the sacrificial safety of known?

Who do you turn to
when no other has come around?
Is it for the hoping that life will bring new dreams
or the birth of acceptance
when you acknowledge you are All.

- (Anniversary, August 2008)

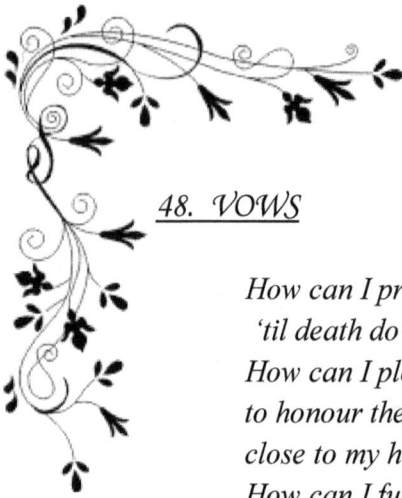

48. VOWS

How can I promise
'til death do us part?
How can I pledge
to honour thee and to hold you
close to my heart?
How can I fulfil
life's superficial vows?
How can I then live true
straight from the start?

Only by being faithful
to destinies call
committing my soul fully
to honour the All.

You and I chose
before space and time
to live and to love
without endorsing a crime.

Wholly and eternally
we will endeavour to be
completely united

and ever to see
that which we sprang from
that which we feel
combined not by chains
ready to fly
forever
together
free.

- (Anniversary, August 2008)

49. JUSTICE

Would it be honourable
for souls' existence
to discriminate
love
by
colour
creed
race
or
gender
would it be surreal
to love
by
denying
it
truth?

Sophisticated philosophers
deviant thieves
tormented mind

I ask you
why you
filtrate life
rewarding
perceived peasants
with
nothingness.

50. *DEBRIS*

If silence could
alter sustenance
and suppression
monitor pain
would that not
then
create
change?

If change could
frail thread
and lifelessness
bring breath
would that not
then
create
trust?

If trust could
Heal pus
and love
produce life
would that not
then
create
another lie?

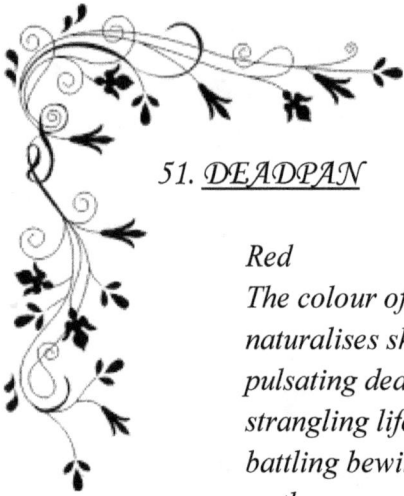

51. DEADPAN

Red
The colour of anger
naturalises sky
pulsating deaths creed
strangling life's molecules
battling bewilderedly
as the sun
removes the veil.

51. *INVITATION*

Come paint with me
'til we sense the essence of the constituencies,
Come dance with me
'til we ascend the existence of the composition,
come laugh with me
'til we vibrate the sustenance of emotion.
who are we 'til we have acknowledged our
fragmented distortion?

Love me –that's hard
Feel me – that's cold
Sense me- that's hurt
Be me – you will know the truth

Hidden
beneath,
make-up,
sacrificial heroine
flying yonder
as I lay my head
beneath
satin comfort
and smile

Hear me not!

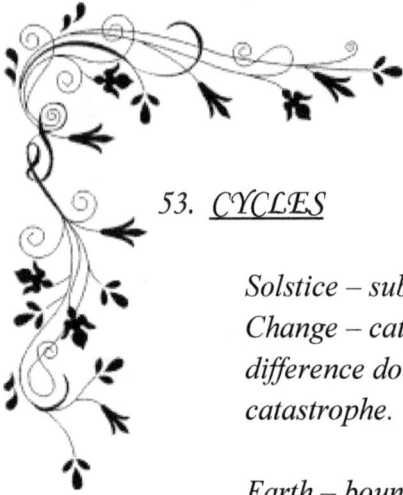

53. CYCLES

Solstice – substantial,
Change – catastrophic
difference doeth depend on substance of the
catastrophe.

Earth – boundaries
Soul – eternal
Death doeth depend on barriers of eternity.

Streams – flow
Water – dependable
on life's liquid forms.
Depending is endless
until you accept to let it go

54. *SOLICITATION*

Behind societies sanitised sanity,
I find my own madness that stares me in the eyes
and smiles,
as I triumphantly march into the depth of its war
cry and scream victoriously.

Who are we without Self?
What have they made us?
Never will we surrender and sacrifice earth's
truths...
The matter.

- (01 December 2008)

55. <u>BETRAYAL</u>

If I lay you down and spoke words of truth
would you still love and hold me gently in your
mind?

If I uttered words of reality
would you still kiss these lips of mine?

If all failed and I exposed my nakedness
 would you still cherish my exposure?

Life is flawless if the diamond is untouched by
mans made theories,
and sins are annulled
because language is just.

56. DON'T

Don't capture my yearnings to find myself,
they're too confusing and illogical to label and
display upon your shelf.
Actions that I perform are not the norm
but according to whom?
It is I who decides and that is all you should
consume.

Life is but an illusion
We are only travellers passing through
So don't try stop me journeying
And I will not you.

Don't analyse my actions
I only yearn to be true to myself
I'm too confusing and illogical
to be displayed upon your shelf.
Actions I perform may not be normal
but according to whom?
Is it not I who decides –
and that's all I wish you to consume.
Life is but an illusion –
we are only but travellers passing through,
so please don't try stop my journey
and I will neither you.
- (08 December 2008)

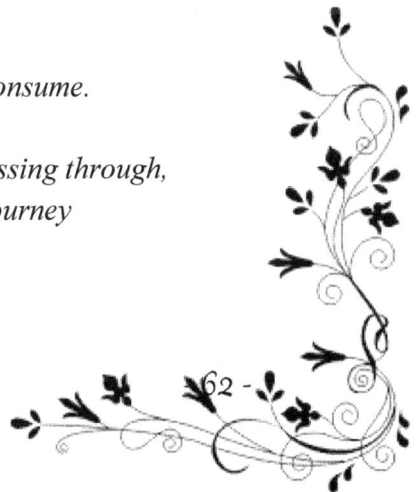

57. SINFUL?

Restricted lovers lie embraced
as they resentfully withhold their desires,
knowing that they may not partake
because of humans' superficial law.
His hardness aches for her pulsating organs,
but no actions they may perform.
His hair entwines her un-naked breasts
while his hands clench out for all.
Her sealed lips scream silently,
will they ever be truthfully heard?
True lovers they should be,
but powerlessly they sacrifice destiny's call.

58. SUBSTRATUM

Moments may come and they may go,
memories of that one moment is what I cling to.
Sensations may alter or they may abide,
Substituting our past familiarities,
in solitude I cried,
not for return of reminiscence nor for cure,
only for pain to substantiate that which was
indeed pure.

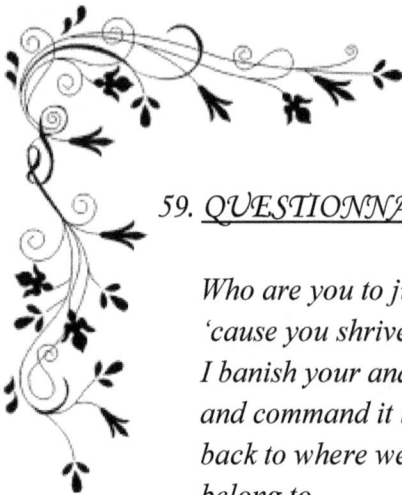

59. QUESTIONNAIRE?

Who are you to judge my sanity,
'cause you shrivel up and choke in own pride.
I banish your analytical, cynical, parasitical verdict
and command it to fly free,
back to where we all stem from,
belong to,
and will forever one day will be.
There non-judgmentally, purely you will find - that
which you condemned is reflecting three fold back to
thee.

60. CRUCIFIED

I searched for love
they gave me a ring of chains.
I carried the burdens
of superficial replacements
and smiled.

I screamed for freedom
they gave me glass of vinaigrette
to take away my thirst
for unconditional acceptance
and sighed.

I prayed for forgiveness
'they know not who we truly are'
then flew forever
and never died.

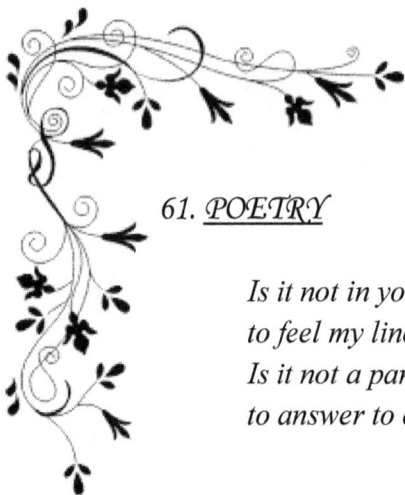

61. <u>POETRY</u>

Is it not in your intellect,
to feel my lines of pain?
Is it not a part of your calibre,
to answer to emotions call?

Line after line
I beckon for you my love to hear,
not my rhythm nor my rhyme,
but for you to catch me
while I fall.

62. <u>FROGS</u>

By listening
I hear the unspoken language of love.

Non-verbal to mankind
croaking life's truths
unconditionally
- life supreme.

Set me free from pledge!

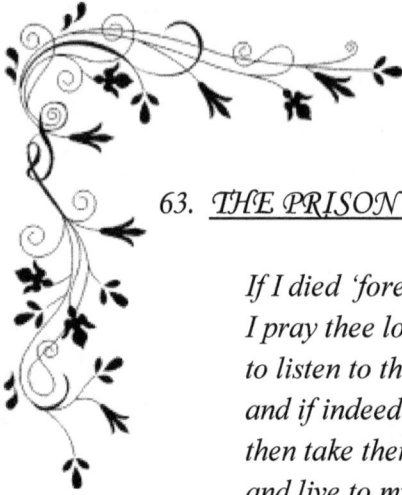

63. THE PRISON CELL

If I died 'fore you awoke,
I pray thee lover
to listen to the words that I wrote
and if indeed you understood my note,
then take them yonder
and live to my hearts cry
of how I felt 'bout mans utter madness.
Go within to find out what I lacked
And liberate minds prison
and bring its sanity back.

64. SKIT

"Oh my god," he cried
"you're married what a shame!
I cannot love thee,
you must live to your husband's beck and call.
Why did you flutter into my life and think I'd fall?
You're beautiful, sensual, utterly define, but now I
excuse myself 'fore we commit a crime."
"Oh no please wait, if only for a moment,
then I shall explain from where I faulted.
Not 'cause of you nor your presence,
but by discriminately relinquishing my name I
altered."
"How should I believe your flirtatious tune,
'cause you are woman and I the ruler?
Wilt thou not ponder on thou irresponsible behaviour
once night turns to light and discover the crueller?"
"That I'd do gladly if you'd allow me one glimpse,
not of shadow nor body of mind,
Ejaculate my soul and set us both free.
Journey jointly and I will repay thee in kind."

65. BIRTHDAY

I've watched your body grow older,
Yet the memories of our intertwined souls
 will never change.
The love you've shown unconsciously have
proven love's ultimate arrange.
As we develop from day to day,
nothing can ever alter,
it's not the body or brain or matter
but 'cause to us life is never strange.

66. DISTILLED

Golden spirit of perfumed purity,
Liquefy my thirst in years of tranquil distillation.
Transcend time of youth and sanity.
Take away my minds anxiety,
Set its force free to soar with eagles.
Let it never be untrue
to that which it's made of,
from which I am,
unprocessed and distilled by natures' hand.

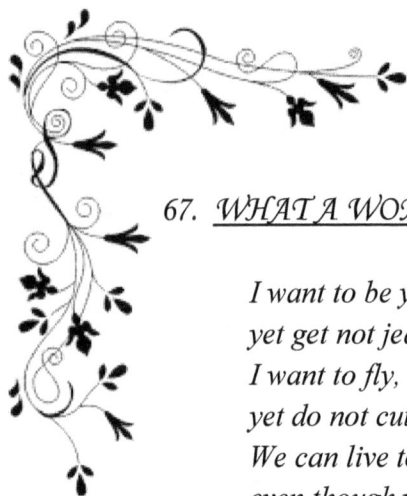

67. <u>WHAT A WOMAN WANTS</u>

I want to be your woman,
yet get not jealous of another.
I want to fly,
yet do not cut these satin wings.
We can live together,
even though we dance out of sync.
Who cares how high the distress gathers,
as long as you
and you alone,
are the fairy queen's lover?

68. _PALETTE_

I tried to paint pictures on canvas that displayed
my soul,
colours of array could not capture the disarray.
Found pen then paper and freedom of my mind,
so take it as it comes and in it yourself you'll find,
not the palette, nor its verb,
only substance of life's real matter can be heard.

Deaf, blind and dumbness,
paralysed to numbness,
he or she who seeks the sustenance,
will feel the longing and become the essence
far yonder from this lie.

Reach within and together we can fly,
not with wings, jets or matter,
only by altering our minds state of flutter.
There we will blindly believe,
in reality that we receive.

Fires will freeze,
and winds become a breeze,
nightingales have wings,
together all sings,
to the tune of nothingness,
and life begins.

All words and phrases that we seek to hide,
can 'come deeply rooted and untouched by life's
tide.

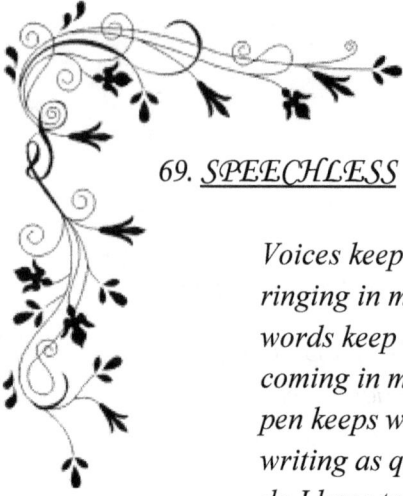

69. SPEECHLESS

Voices keep ringing,
ringing in my head,
words keep coming,
coming in my head,
pen keeps writing,
writing as quick as light,
do I have to utter these thoughts too?

What, why, who or where
are not delectable phrases offered to me.
Sick of logic,
tired of death,
show me now another.

70. EYES SHUT OPEN

And after the day is done
I sit in silence and ponder
'bout what's achieved
and what's gained
and realise it does not really matter
'cause the day is gone
and the essence of dew
will bring newness
to those that accomplish
the transitional status
of being a part
of the metamorphic status
of human embracement.

So as I lay my head to rest
these eyes I close
and touch my shadows of moments past
knowing fully that time is only sustenance
of mans mind and state

I am not them
they do not really care
so the altered sate
beckons me
to return tonight.

71. <u>POLKA DOTS</u>

Grooming an outfit for any occasion
is essential
'cause the frog you once kissed
might just become the prince
who amends himself
and expects his female
to be in the perfect garment
and ready,
well prepared
safe to eat
untreated
Sterilised
screwed.

Part 2

AN INTRODUCTION TO PART TWO POETRY

Meeting our Marriage Councillor/ Life Coach in the early months of 2009, brought me into a new phase of my life's journey. Nancy I wish to thank you for walking alongside during this cynical part of my timeframe. You often carried me while I was too weak to think, tugged me when the phobias held me back, and yet in the end taught me to find the light in the darkness! I want to dedicate these poems to you, my spiritual sister, as each one was written during this segment of my life's journey.

"Thank you Nancy Grover for believing in me."

72. _NANCY_

Nancy you don't understand what you are
opening up,
Why should I listen to you!
You are neither my god nor the goddess,
So what the fuck do you care!
Why should I deal with it?
Will you see the puss I suck?
Will you be emotionally exposed?
Will I undress my life on a canvas?
But I will paint, and paint, and paint
For those who caused my pain
So that an imprint of societies sick fucked minds
Can stare it in face
And cut away their sophisticated side

I will not surrender
Even though I died
I am messenger
Of the wounded womanhood's pride

- (15 April 2009)

73. DREAMS

If tomorrow never arrived
I would know,
and remember-
that I lived my dream
Finding you.

- Circle whole

Thank you for loving me so unconditionally,
thank you for making me so complete

- (16 April 2009)

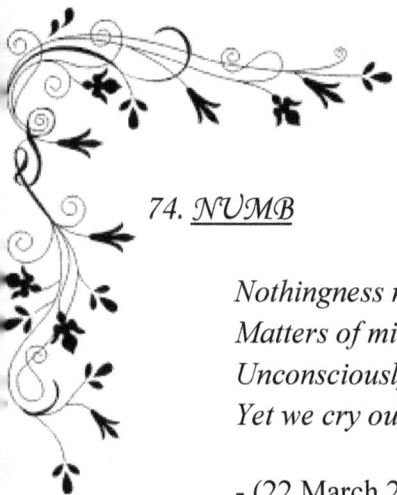

74. *NUMB*

Nothingness nullifies our conditional confusions
Matters of mind drown our destiny
Unconsciously we are ALL –
Yet we cry out for only more pain

- (22 March 2009)

75. <u>PUPPET</u>

Jeans removed
A demo I became
as the audience applauded
the presentation of my virgin thighs
Bring it on,
let me resonate your thrills,
appraise your perversions,
that lust in mind
For five minutes you will observe your sexual
desires.
Will they satisfy and remain in your memory
'til the day you die?
Do you live now and still remember?
Have you satisfied your momentary pleasure,
or will you never want to know
'bout the girl that you stripped,
raped and hurt forever-
all in innocence
and then prayed to your god?

76. _ASPHYXIATED_

Stuff these subconscious thoughts
Stuff society
Stuff life
Stuff death
Stuff everything
- I will become free.

The chains that once held me
The lies that I once heard
The hurts that made me bleed
The creatures that once lived in this head
I banish you into your own darkness
To suffocate to nothingness

Burn you all
I am FREE

- (17 April 2009)

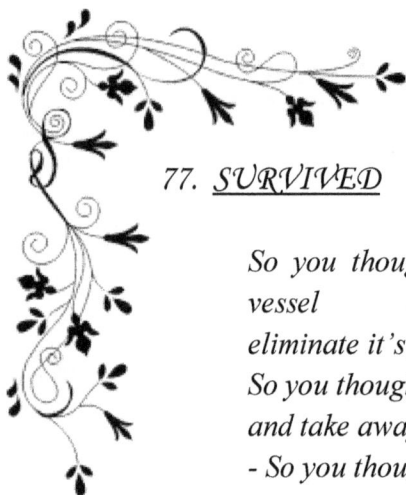

77. <u>SURVIVED</u>

So you thought you could break my porcelain
vessel
eliminate it's finely tuned frequency.
So you thought you could erase my palette
and take away it's pastel textured constituency
- So you thought.

This soul still lives to fight for forgiveness
and sound it's sinless solstice servitude
it will paint new life
while feeding off thoughts of love
and create life to become another
exactly like it was
and always was
meant to be

- (17 April 2009)

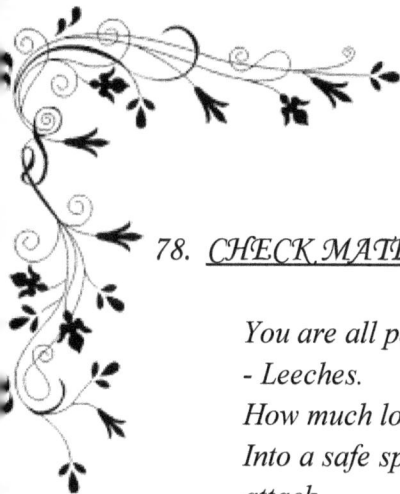

78. CHECK MATE

You are all parasitic suckers,
- Leeches.
How much longer must you fuck with my mind?
Into a safe space I will observe your every tactful
attack
and annihilate them strategically one by one
'til your tongue is numb
'til your breath is clenched
'til your eyes are hollow
'til your ears are pierce
Fuck you too.

- (20 April 2009)

79. GLUTTONY

We need so little to make us satisfied,
Yet we strive for more each day.
Soul yearns to be watered
Yet we prick our own fear.

Searching without expectations
brings us closer to True Source
nothing out there is dearer
than touching our own Truth

- (22.04.2009)

80. COLONY

What if
one day
we
realised
that the stones we worked for
had become
suffocating
layers of cement
and that
we
had buried
our truths of love
beneath?

- (22 April 2009)

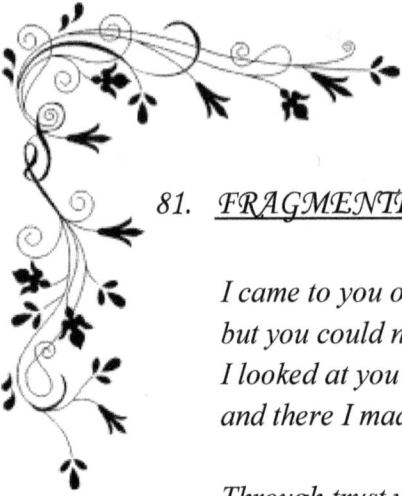

81. FRAGMENTED VASE

I came to you on sale,
but you could not afford my price.
I looked at you deeply,
and there I made my sacrifice.

Through trust we would progress,
together we would reap the rewards,
through thick and thin I would be your treasure,
and become like a lady amongst the lords

Taking me home to your humble base,
you shone and cleaned your array
and then one day you threw me onto concrete floor,
and bought another with the flowers I once did
display.

- (28 April 2009)

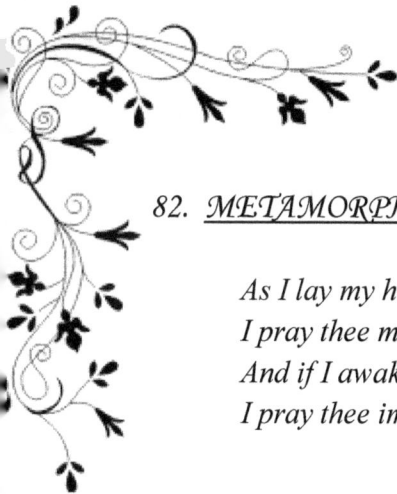

82. *METAMORPHOSIS*

As I lay my head to hide
I pray thee mind to clean
And if I awake before it doeth
I pray thee immortal soul to fly

- (28 April 2009)

83. <u>*RESTORATION*</u>

Time is like a rose
blooming yet withers to nothingness
and leaves its petals
to tell its story
Marks of time…
Memories
Fresh
Dying
Withered
Discarded

- (28 April 2009)

84. *STILT*

High heal shoes
wear their tear
as they heed
to societies beck and call

Stride by stride
they step deeper
as they sophistically
shine their array
Yet true love slithers
to find sanity
and hide its feet away

- (28 April 2009)

85. <u>*DESIRES*</u>

I want to fly like wind
Love like sun
Shine like stars
Radiate like fire
Feel like earth
And be loved and love
deep and forever

Encaged by numbed emotions
She stares lifelessly into the icy atmosphere
that diabolically embraces her mind
Ticking heart pulsates time
Claustrophobic soul
Sentenced to live

- (03 May 2009)

86. THE UNFORGIVEN

Gracefully they plucked her feathers,
One by one
Soaked body in salt
Seasoned with royal spices
Cooked at 180 for 60 minutes
Ate
And smiled

Her soul looked down
And whispered
"Forgive them mother, they know not what
they've done"

- (July 2008)

87. WOMAN

Designated powers,
control identification
Roll call solutes my name
Stepping forward
I place my thumb
Into the contaminated ink pad
And mark my being

88. FRIDAY THE THIRTEENTH

Have I become so emotionless,
that I have forgotten 'bout pain?
You cry yet I don't know how to tap into your
realm
You hurt and I become that 'nothing' that altered
my being.
Do I live in a monarchy,
that no other can understand,
or am I so detached,
that your aches,
are no longer a part of my calibre?
Sorry my baby
I wish I could rock your tears away,
but the cradle strings have long time snapped,
and now you need to fly.
Hopefully one day,
if the Great Creator destines our paths to cross
again,
we can run naked in the rain,
and "see" what we have lost.

You are beautiful,
and your love was given conditionally.
There was joy in my heart,
when I recalled our past,
maybe someday we will be
united,
 yet free.
But for now get lost.

89. INDISSOLUBLE?

Fucking punish me,
Hit me,
Hit me more,
I don't care.
Come on you asshole,
see how many more lines,
can leave a scar.
More, more, more
Come on show me what you made of
Am I weak?
Is that what you want to prove?
Curse me with your tongue,
Accuse me I beg,
Come on fuck-head,
show me how load,
how deep,
you can penetrate my mind.

Scream, scream,
Please scream louder,
Is that your best shot?
Punish me,
Fucking do what you want,
Fuck you all,
I hate you all too much.

Tried to be the light and love,
- but now fuck you all,
You've sucked enough blood,
I will hide in the darkest hole,
I'm not coming out any more.

Pain is good,
I carry your burdens,
Stripes of blood to heal your sins,
Blood, blood fucking blood,
Life to you all,
You want blood?
Come get it,
I'll show you,
Fucking blood.

Why,
What,
How,
Who,
When,
Reason?
There is no goddam reason.
Why choose me to give me fucking pain?
I don't feel the pain,
Leave me alone that's what I want,
I can carry my own cross

Bring it on,
Send those thoughts,
Mail your pus filled mentalities,
Send them my way.
Come on,
Are you scared?
Do you think you might hurt my fucking feelings?
Do you actually care?
Curse me,
Fucking try.
You cannot even pierce my mind,
Is there any sanity actually left?
Find it,
Find it
I beg you please,
And if you do,
And when you do,
Take it away too.
So fuck you,
Go scream more.

- (03 February 2010)

90. CHILD OF LIGHT?

So you thought you could slowly strangle sanity?
You wanted it to be so perfect,
Now come and find a light in my darkness.
Who am I?
Not even a reflection of you?
You fucking moulded me into your tormented
reality,
Broke me so I now conform

- (03 February 2010)

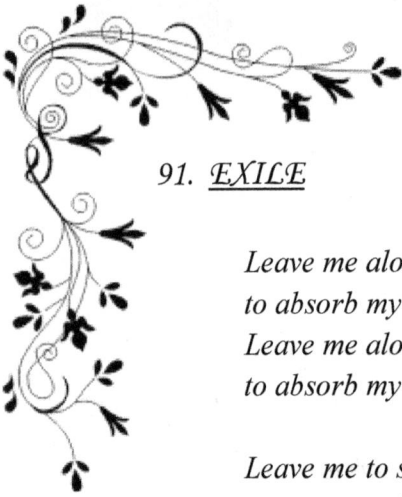

91. EXILE

Leave me alone in silence,
to absorb my insanity.
Leave me alone in insanity,
to absorb my silence.

Leave me to stare,
into my own blackness.
Leave me in emptiness,
to drink the taste.

Leave me to cut,
into my bodily flesh,
leave me in it's pulse,
to feel my own pain.

Now leave me alone,
now leave me alone,
now leave me alone,
let me be my judge

- (05 February 2010)

92. MORTIFIED

The first cry of birth,
indicates life
The last sigh of life,
indicates death

in innocence we are born,
then moulded to conform,
to the rigid rules of humankind,
who crush our dreams,
cut our wings,
wipe away our smiles,
and tread upon our truths.

What is there to live for,
when we already know the end?
What is there to die for,
when we already experience death?

- (12 February 2010)

93. OUR FATHER?

Forgive me father,
If I have sinned,
Forgive me mother,
If I have cried,
Forgive me all,
If I have died.

- (12 February 2010)

94. _JUSTIFY_

Is it just
to live a lie
when the truth
suppresses your blood?

Is it just
to breathe in air
when the vapour
smells like dust?

Is it just
to wake at dawn
when the dream
alters life itself?

Is it just
to walk a path
when the blades of grass
slash only scars?

Is it just
to fake a smile
when the lines
dig graves unseen?

Tell me please
Is it just?

- (13 February 2010)

95. *DO OR DIE*

No substitute
No loss
No failure
While I am alive
I will live

- (17 February 2010)

- Part 3 -

And now through His grace I am free - Free to find the "forgotten" me.
My journey continues each new day. I choose only life, love and light and celebrate my uniqueness.
I am a free being but a part of the ALL.

96. _WHAT IS LOVE?_

Love is a wind,
that embraces your soul
with its gentle breeze.

Love is a sun,
that nurtures your mind
with its radiant breeze.

Love is a bird,
that resonates your being
with its melody

- (20 February 2010)

97. *THE DAY MOON LAY UPSIDE DOWN*

Staring up for reasons,
while aching down inside
Who had caused these changes of seasons?
Why had all hopes died?

Life commitment now broken,
We removed our marriage token
Tears swam down face
All that remains now
Will come by His Grace.

- (21 February 2010)

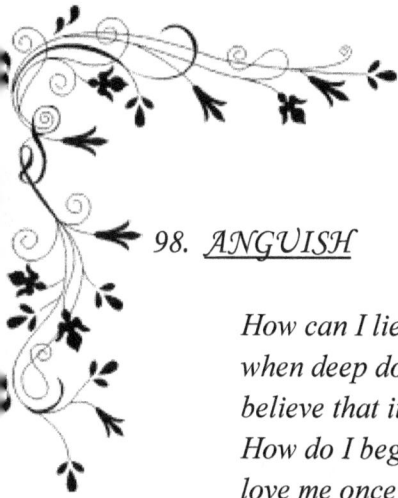

98. ANGUISH

How can I lie and say that the pain is no more,
when deep down my soul burns and longs to
believe that it was only a dream.
How do I begin to lift up my spirit and reach to
love me once again,
when the truth is my heart yearns to re-love that
which we have lost.

Was it love?
Was it pain?
Was it real
or an illusion?
What is love?
What is pain?
What is real and not real?

My mind now too confused to think of
conclusions
My heart now too broken to feel the delusions
We can only believe that next life we reconnect
Believing in oneness and having no regret
The emptiness engulfs my body,
Yet the torrents of tears cannot cleanse my
anguish,
I am left with not even hope

that things may one day be restored
'cause we have tried, and lied and died
only to find that each time we return to question
our choices,

our wounds re-opened and spurt out pain, acid
blood and fears.
Leave sleeping dogs to rest,
Leave cats to spill their milk
Leave life to be
I now set you completely free.

My body now too tired to feel illusions
My senses now too clogged to paint impressions
Hold onto the magic in which we once believed
As humans we failed and through that deceived.

- (22 April 2010)

99. THE DEAD LOVER

Staring into icy blue eyes
I caress your lifeless body
Clenching on to your nothingness
I stroke away your death

Echoes of my screams
clutch to the hollow walls.
    No longer can you feel my words,
Your blood has turned to ice
No longer can you feel my pain
Your body is now lame.

Why my God did he have to die?
Could we not have shared just one last day?
Why are you so cruel that you took him away?
    So many questions,
The pain too deep to pray
What should I live for,
Why should I care?

Is this my punishment,
Or is this the prize?

Life grows into mourning,
As the maggots feed on my soul
Day time is blackened

by the warmth of my blood.

Pray open my eyes to see the world of united
souls
where I can become whole
and live while I die.

- (22 April 2010)

100. *SAVIOUR?*

An addict I am,
I crave my abusive fix.
Hurts and pains
For them I ache

Give me just one last shot,
I need it so badly,
I accept your syringe,
to inject it under my skin gladly
Please, please I beg of thee
nothing else in this life can ever satisfy me
without you I will truly die,
Imagine if I found out 'bout love,
or become light and shone and smiled
Please, please I beg you to give it to me
I honestly can feel I cannot be free
Eternally I have become your martyr and
devotee.

- (22 April 2010)

101. CLOSED CHAPTER

When does a woman close the chapter of her
broken hearts tale,
Can she ever accept the emptiness if she
releases her deepest scars?
Will she ever begin to breastfeed her own
inner child,
Knowing that the milk was given to him and
now run dry?
What is it she is essentially searching for,
After she has come to the conclusion that life
is in actual fact a farce?
How can she start dancing and believing in
love once more,
When he has walked out and left her to lie in
her own pool of tears?
Does she have the strength to pick up the
broken pieces and throw them all away,
Can she stitch up the wounds and make it
through another day?
Why should she feel worthy if she was once
bitten and now become shy,
Who will she nurture or should she lay down
and just die?

102. *DO YOU STILL BELIEVE IN?*

When in doubt and we are far apart,
Look to the stars and there you will find,
the little fairy that once believed and loved
you
straight from her childlike heart.

She was never really truly understood,
and she often questioned why,
but she lived to fulfil one life's purpose,
knowing that all other things would in time
surely die.

Seeing him before her one Friday afternoon,
She gazed into his eyes so gentle, kind and
blue,
realised that this was the soul that she had
been searching for,
    he was the one for her
Soon she would free him -
together fly higher than the highest moon.

    But he loved and then left her,
to bring them back jewels of pain,
She had no option but to release him,
soon he would learn there was no truth in
material gain.

At night she lay awake insane,
Hoping for him to soon return,
Time dragged to months,
months grew to years,
'til eventually she could take no further
She screamed to forces from the other
worlds,
and cried out for love in innocence name.

No more could she bear
So she packed her bags to find the road
to her lost love that she once knew.
Where had he disappeared,
Why had their love died -
'cause when they met it had seemed so true?

With wand in hand,
And hope and love as her guide,
She ventured to another land
 knowing that by believing in light, truth and
love
he would soon hold her close back by his
side.

This story is a long one,
It ended like most sad books do,

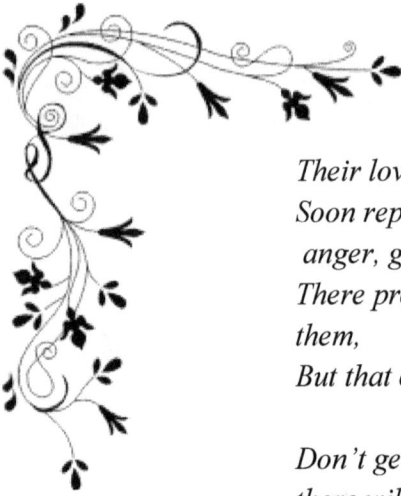

Their love was lost forever,
Soon replaced by logical conclusions,
 anger, greed and pride.
There probably will be no second chance for
them,
But that only that fairy's fate will decide.

Don't get me wrong this does not mean that
there will be no other
'cause her true purpose was to be a real
lover
she came to shine light and walk in magic
like most fairies do,
Why would she give up now when there
really are so few?

Magic, magic, magic,
she waved her wand up high
asked the above to bring her a new light-
being
to take back to her true home in the sky

     And so the story goes on and on and on...
Forever.

Fairies may come and they may go,
But when you find that one that truly loves
you,
Makes sure you keep her safe in your heart,

Cause there she will stay and believe in
never being apart

Magic, magic, magic,
she waves her wand up high
asks the above to bring a new being
to take back to her other home way up in the
sky.

The moral of the fairy tale story,
Don't cut her wings too short,
Allow her the freedom to fly in her world
'cause there she will shine and make you her
pride and glory.

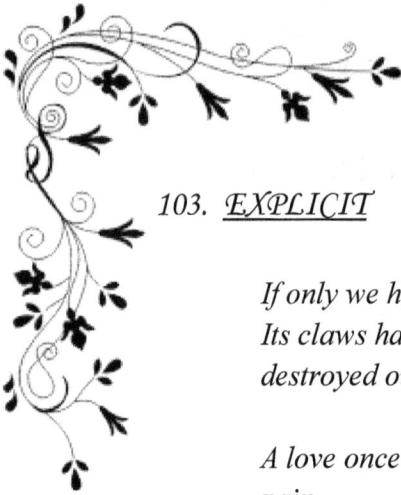

103. *EXPLICIT*

If only we had not become victims of society,
Its claws have clenched our truths;
destroyed our Wholeness.

A love once deep now lies splattered by scars of
pain.
We believed it would last forever
but now hide from one another
yet pray that time will separate distance and
reunite us once again.

- (11 September 2010)

104. WHAT IS LOVE

Love is the touch of two hands;
Combining as One.
Love is the knowing that All is everything,
And everything is All.
Love is the Spirit that smells the petals of its
seed.

If a painter could paint a portrait to express
Love,
It would take a lifetime – have no beginning or
ending.
If a musician could play a tune,
It would resonate notes unheard by ear but felt
by soul.

- (10 September 2010)

105. _CHESS_

Are you content now,
do you feel you've won the Game?

The king stands alone on his board that has
been so logically carved.

Does he have feelings,
does he long for his queen?

Has he sacrificed his emotions to prove he has
All –
but alas nothing.

- (11 September 2010)

106. CARCASS

Cut skin and bled
Cried life and died
Sucked air and choked
Seen blackness and did not care

What more must I give, live, strive for if my very
essence of existence beats no more?
Is it for dreams or expectations from others,
What more must I sigh for
if only death is my wish

www.ingramcontent.com/pod-product-compliance
Lightning Source LLC
Chambersburg PA
CBHW060511030426
42337CB00015B/1850